Sufficiency of the Actual

Books by Kevin Stein

Poetry
Sufficiency of the Actual (2009)
American Ghost Roses (2005)
Chance Ransom (2000)
Bruised Paradise (1996)
A Circus of Want (1992)

Criticism
Private Poets, Worldly Acts (1996)
James Wright: The Poetry of a
Grown Man (1989)

Anthologies
Bread & Steel, audio CD (2007)
Illinois Voices, edited with
G. E. Murray (2001)

Sufficiency of the
Actual

Poems by
KEVIN STEIN

University of Illinois Press
Urbana and Chicago

© 2009 by Kevin Stein
All rights reserved
Manufactured in the United States of America
1 2 3 4 5 C P 5 4 3 2 1

♾ This book is printed on acid-free paper.

Library of Congress Cataloging-in-Publication Data
Stein, Kevin
Sufficiency of the actual : poems / by Kevin Stein.
    p.   cm. — (Illinois poetry series)
ISBN 978-0-252-03309-4 (cloth : alk. paper)
ISBN 978-0-252-07600-8 (pbk. : alk. paper)
I. Title.
PS3569.T3714S84   2008
811'.54—dc22   2008012686

For Deb,

For Kirsten & Joseph

Contents

Acknowledgments

Several poems in this manuscript have appeared previously in journals. Grateful acknowledgment is made to the following magazines: *American Letters & Commentary*: "Lovesong Ending with (   )." *Arts and Letters*: "Appetites Earthly and Other," "Mars' Karma," and "Postcard to Henry James." *Big Muddy:* "Parakeet and Dark Star," "Pre-Bowdlerized Version of Poem for a Fourth-Grade Illinois History Text," and "Thinking of the Second Time They Shoveled Up Mr. Lincoln." *Boulevard*: "Aesthetics of Desire," "Lives of the Painters," and "Slippery Slope." *Collage*: "Poet's Genie" and "Religion." *Colorado Review*: "September Falls Is No River's." *Crab Orchard Review*: "Middle-aged Adam's and Eve's Bedside Tables" and "In Human Hands." *Ecotone:* "News Crawl" and "Youthful Indiscretions." *Fifth Wednesday*: "Natural Selection," "Post-Feminist Machismo," "Talk Radio," "To Balance," and "Upon the Porch Swing's Time Machine." *Flying Island:* "CR5115STD Responds to the National Consumer Survey." *Fourth River*: "At the Mountain Man Rendezvous, Fairplay, Colorado." *Hayden's Ferry Review*: "Song of the Night Shift Foreman." *The Laurel Review*: "Ike's Caddy." *The North American Review*: "(My) History of Parsley." *OnEarth:* "Mowing the Lawn." *Poetry*: "Arts of Joy," "Autumnal," and "Sufficiency of the Actual." *Poetry East*: "Inverse Aviary, in which Birds Talk." *The Southern Review*: "Blue Tuesday" and "Capitalism." *Sou'wester*: "To My Hair." *TriQuarterly*: "Colonialism," "On Being a Nielsen Family," and "Parable of the American Stag Party."

"Pre-Bowdlerized Version of Poem for a Fourth-Grade Illinois History Text" appears, Bowdlerized, as "Your Illinois" in *Illinois Studies* (Boston: Houghton-Mifflin, 2006). "Sufficiency of the Actual" is heard on the audio compact disk, *Bread & Steel: Illinois Poets Reading from Their Works* (Café Press, 2007). The opening line of "In Human Hands" owes to Keith Ratzlaff's "The Body Pledges Its Allegiance" from *Man Under a Pear Tree* (Anhinga Press, 1997). "Inverse Aviary, in which Birds Talk" draws from C. K. Williams' *The Lark. The Thrush. The Starling. (Poems from Issa)*; see Williams' *Selected Poems* (Farrar, Straus, and Giroux, 1994). "Ike's Caddy" is dedicated to Clint McCown, who toted the bag.

I am grateful for Bradley University's generous support, which offered time to write some of these poems, and for the Illinois Arts Council's naming "Middle-aged Adam's and Eve's Bedside Tables" its 2007 Literary Award winner. For the balm of their friendship and of their poetry, I am indebted to Keith Ratzlaff, Dean Young, Clint McCown, Jeff Gundy, Jeff Knorr, David Wojahn, Tony Hoagland, and Bob Hicok. Thanks to Professors Crowe, Fuller, and Teeven for inventive instructional support. Thanks as well to Laurence Lieberman for the benefit of his editor's eye and ear. Thanks to Jimmy's high corner tables, front and rear. Thanks to Lily and AllFlash NoCash+ for admission to their realms. Thanks to Kirsten and Joseph for their fine songs. Thanks to Deb for the grace of her blue-eyed yes.

"History's . . . the conversation that we are."
    —*Hans-Georg Gadamer*

"If you know your history,
 you will know where you're coming from.
 You won't have to ask me,
 'Who the hell is Abraham?'"
    —*Bob Marley*

One

Autumnal

Lofting the Molotov cocktail into the church's
empty lot was, in retrospect, a political act.
Back then it was only three guys I didn't like
unhanding the girly mags, fevered to spectacular action.
Friday night and no driver's license gave us this license.

In the graveyard we slunk behind granite markers,
thumbing cloth down the Coke bottle's high octane throat.
Strange, how doing something marks your life,
hard and permanent as stone, as years later,
driving home from the hospital after something

they called our baby had died, I thought I'd turned
the corner when no I'd not. It had turned on me.
Wittgenstein says you can't see the periphery
of your world because you're in it. He penciled
a sketch in his *Tractatus* just to prove it, buddy,

which is what, in a way, the cops said to me.
Molotov, what's it like to have a weapon named after you?
You're the world's word for insurrection. Emerson says
words themselves are actions, though bless him,
in his dotage he forgot even how to ask for a glass of _____.

Some words you can't say without invoking action.
Against them, there's cultural or moral injunction,
but "dead baby" you say only in the bathroom
with the water running. It's what's not said each time
you blow out the candle. It's what nothing's named after.

Some things you do you wish you hadn't.
Some you don't you wish you had.
It's years before you know the difference,
so what good's remorse? At the hospital
with my wife, what prayer could I have spoken

to what forgetful god? In time, we break things,
stupid and unreflective. In time, we're broken
by things, stupid and unreflective. After I'd tossed
the Molotov, I ran like water through dark alleys.
I never looked back for flames I didn't believe in either.

Sufficiency of the Actual

Had I freed the one-legged cricket twitching in the roses'
        spider-webbed twilight,
I'd become Patron Saint of One-Legged Crickets Twitching
        in Spider-Webbed Twilight.
I'd be Saint of Cracked Song, Patron of the Incomplete
        and Longing.
But then, saintly though I might be, the spider goes hungry.

Anyway, there's already a multitude, patrons of the broken web,
        unrisen bread,
lost keys—so many, this book says, their duties overlap, say,
        Patron Saint of Fractions.
(See Incomplete and Longing.) That's who The Who prayed to,
        trashing instruments
as "Pop Art Auto Destruction," this, Pete Townsend's phrase,

his name a line and demarcation. The young like to break things,
        even themselves.
The young like a summer drum you put your foot through:
        thump worship.
Jon Entwistle, The Who's bassist, stored all his parts
        in a wooden
coffin box, until middle-age donned its knee-high socks.

Then he undid the undoing, cobbling five guitars into one
        he dubbed "Frankenstein,"
whose name my friend Frank and I shared with it and, well,
        with Wollstonecraft's
romantic sci-fi tragic victim hero. Together, we made a creature
        the smarty pants party drunks
called "Frank-and-Stein" from the keg-drenched kitchen.

Aren't we all cobbled of pieces, glued and screwed and strung
        together,
ready to snap? Are we instruments some huge hand plucks?
        Are we the roses
or a cricket's cracked song? And redemption?—in the end
        Entwistle's estate
auctioned "Frankenstein" for a cool $100,000.

Frank did ten years in the county orphanage. (See Incomplete
        and Longing).
His mother remarried a furnace whose pilot wouldn't stay lit.
        You've heard about
the stutterer who falling from a ladder is cured of his affliction
        but made suddenly
blind. What he no longer sees he sings about instead.

On Being a Nielsen Family

We pocket five ones when we agree,
fingered cash our soul's ransom.
And a Family Viewership Record Book
for each TV, of which we've three.
We are the Postmodern Descartes,

pledging, "I watch, therefore I am."
We're the grand experiment that was
America, both scientist and the mouse
with a human ear stitched to its pink back,
checking the appropriate idiot-box boxes.

We're our own Peeping Tom, peering in.
On stage, we're culture's disguise,
the way a bickering couple makes nice
once the bell ding-dongs neighbors in
for cocktails and unsalted Cheese Nips.

Though we watch *Oprah,* we circle *BBC News.*
Though it's *Jerry Springer,* we mark *Charlie Rose.*
No no no. Not *South Park,* not *Cops,*
not World's Funniest Animal Tricks,
but History Channel and Discovery,

NASA Live, *Nightline,* and Devotionals,
the Food Network's Thanksgiving Day
Vegan Special. We are watched watching,
watching ourselves watched. We are never
enough, so the lie is as we wish to be.

(My) History of Parsley

"That reminds me of the time" is one way the boring
prove themselves so, absconding with a conversation
as a thief might the chicken thrust under his coat,

trusting we'll overlook our story's ruffled feathers,
all that clucking, an occasional foot cleaving
yellow air for some firm purchase it won't get.

Herodotus, the Father of History, never once uttered
"that reminds me of the time" to thus swerve from
kingly battle to his own troubles with an ill-tempered goat.

But we mere mortals love most our own story,
no doubt the reason I've drifted shamefully from
the herbalist lecturing how apiol's the volatile oil

responsible for parsley's healing properties.
It's written brave Hercules wove parsley garlands,
hence those victory crowns centuries old but recently

fallen from favor. It's no myth Greeks fed parsley
to quicken race horses and chomped fistfuls themselves,
oral hygiene after feasts of lamb and much garlic.

Not to be outdone, English parents fibbed
babies came from parsley beds. That's one white lie
with a sprig of truth if lovers munched parsley

to cleanse the stench of their table's dark fare,
then off to bed. That reminds me of the time
my wife cut a clutch of parsley and brought with it

the surprise neon caterpillar, green eagerness
ready to spin its chrysalis in a Ball jar.
All winter waiting waited in our expectant hands.

There now, that's the history of our first born.

drop but my son's name for acorns
    falling from white oak and bur,
        the apples plopping Delicious,
our Cortland's plump thump. You can—
    with risk— walk beneath September Falls
        as you might beneath the watery ones.
Acorns ping through branches, Plinko
    on *The Price Is Right,* but what you win
        just smarts your head. I've never been
    Newton-ed by an apple, but yellowjackets—
those cider-drunk eunuchs—make testy combat
        for the ripe ones still hanging within reach.
    I've never been to war either, which is to be
        not exactly Newton-ed
but plunked in a way more final.
    Our world's lucky not to have been Teller-ed
        by an H-bomb, Edward the "Father of,"
who slept with one eye open
        for the terrible Russians. Radio says
he died today, though probably he died a bit
    when nuking Oppenheimer, his former boss and pal.
Teller, how'd it feel to be hailed the father of maelstrom,
    to plant a deadly seed with your brain and not
        the old fashioned way Stalin's daddy did?
Tomorrow you'll make *The Times*'s obit page,
        merely ink and recycled paper.
From the grave, you'll slaughter legions of innocents,
    or, who knows, save them—your MAD nightmare
        made good as any dream.
For you I'll blow this Morning Glory's trumpet,
    this bloom, Teller, whose blues blow only gold.

News Crawl

Research suggests a gun's *bang bang* is our world's lingua franca.
• Weapon play is tribal, one expert claims. ✿ Local weather on
the 8s. ✿ University studies say our sons strap on goggles to
play "air-soft," waging epic plastic-BB battles across the verdant
lawn. They shoot each other on the run, as men do in Jerusalem
or Fallujah. • Marketing suggests guns make family entertain-
ment. • An unnamed source confirms I've played air-soft, a
lurch of misguided parenting to shoot at one's son. • Reports
speculate some ungodly force makes guns fun. • Can we kill it,
too? • Film at eleven on KNN. • Linguists say the raised fist
with pointed index and thumb shot means, universally, "You're
dead." • It drives me nuts to think of my son with a gun. ✿
Local weather on the 8s. ✿ Nutritionists advise nuts are good
for the heart. • Nuts, critics say, the good father who tries to be
by waving a pistol. • Like father like son. • Tonight's primetime,
a KNN exclusive, features footage of puddled Baghdad blood. •
Studies conclude forgetting is merely a click away.

Mars' Karma

That Mars hiked 60,000 Marches just to brush
his planet's raised sword this close to us
surprises no one who's known hatred's slow simmer.
Why, the Serbs curse battles 600 years past,
and one always expects worse from gods.

True enough, as Mars hurtled nearer,
Joseph's shot on goal sailed wide right.
Mars' Bad Karma, I muttered, recalling the lingo
of college days when blending the pagan and Hindu
made one ecumenical yet groovy.

That's what conquerors do, steal others' gods,
the way Mars himself is really the Greeks' Ares
in nominal disguise. So I blamed everything
on Mars' Bad Karma: a flat tire, the dry well,
our apples' rot, even the squished garden toad.

It didn't stop with the mare's tumor, nor when
the vet knifed it out. "Bad Karma," I screamed
when Karma the stable dog—Bad Karma the stable dog—
ate the tumor right off the stunned vet's bloody scalpel.
Bad Karma's biopsy, Bad Karma's lunch.

No wonder Mars is the bellicose god of war,
something I learned scribbling college notes
just before the Classics prof chose London spring break
to strangle his wife. In his huge-knuckled hands
the chalk stick disappeared except for its yellow tip.

I'd close my eyes and see those hands
around her neck gone limp, glasses knocked off,
how her hair frizzed in London's perpetual drizzle.
The Year of Big Hair, 1976, and Mars had just
departed Vietnam for a hut in Pol Pot's killing fields.

I dumped the Classics minor, blood on my hands.
I dropped the poli sci major, Kissinger's Peace with Honor.
In this way I plotted to hammer a diamond back into coal
and thus start over: "With this lump of coal,
I do unwed thee, brutish world."

Nice try, Mr. T. S. Eliot-Stein. Often we blame
somebody else when that somebody is us.
I drove over that nail and the garden toad too.
Pol Pot planted acres of graves. My prof strangled his wife
in drunken fury. And the Viet Cong launched Tet

so we dropped napalm and My Lai on them.
See, Mars, we're ungodly gods like you.
Who needs your help with the knife? After all,
your son Romulus killed his brother to found Rome.
That proves he was half human.

Lives of the Painters

1
The wisdom of painters, my father claimed,
was to drink too much. Thirst is but one measure
of loss. See Table #10.

2
Above us the universe sighs, doing the Heraclitean slide,
a tune whose chorus we sing by living. Clang clang.
So my brushes felt like wings,
my arms wings,
the whole of me given way to air.

3
The paint can's white mouth, lustrous as if with dew,
mimicked the well-fed Heal All, petal no fool could refuse.
Who could blame the moth splayed there,
Jesus-on-the-cross atop the can's wet kiss,
thirsty, quivering. See Figure #6.

4
Before he died, I painted my father's house,
temple of the home fire.
Money was tight. He'd stopped the *Herald*
and dropped cable.
My mother dyed her own blue hair
and thus her sink blue too.

5
"My Guh, Guh Generation" called it *bread* in bellbottom years,
hip-hugger hip to what money's for. The People.
We'd enough of our parents' smirking.

We'd evolved from "Can't Buy Me Love" to the ceremonial
Summer of.
We wore flowers in our unwashed hair.
What did we know?

6
Yellow on white, the moth floated
death's Post-It note.
All day, and the rungs just tweaked my weak ankles.

7
Queued at Wal-Mart's pill shop,
my father did the Parkinson's quiver,
his rock 'n' roll walk. Muzak's the tune for those who can't get off
the ground except by ladder. *Ibid.*

8
Drunk on ambrosia, the gods slurred,
"Which is our better gift, bread or fire?"

9
My father, Coupon Tuesday's customer #216,
numbered by time and pills,
came to peace with Heraclitus,
who pronounced: "It is not better for humans to get all they want.
It is disease that makes health sweet and good,
hunger satiety, weariness rest."

10
From nothing came the asking, our first language—our wings,
our bread, the temple fire.
From the nothing that came of asking came want,
blue and sputtering as summer's garden hose
raised to parted lips, this kiss.
I wanted the paint-splotched moth to fly.

Middle-aged Adam's and Eve's Bedside Tables

Hers

A deluxe princess phone with snaking cord.
One stopped clock blinking its red eye, 12:01.
E-mail from her Fidelity broker. Abel's baby book.
Mr. Happy, the sore back's best buddy.
Victoria's Secret Miracle Bra missing its left breast cookie.
Tuesday's grocery list: milk, bread, Macintosh.
Her plaster dental mold's cracked smile.
Congealed remains of last night's rib dinner
and her Original No-Sin Low-Fat Cheese Cake.
Empty Cool Whip tub. The Audubon *Book of Trees*.
Friedan's dog-eared *The Feminine Mystique*,
a toppled wine glass. One Applebee's matchbook,
666–2480 scribbled inside. Selected O'Keefe postcards,
orange poppy on top. Here and there, an iris of dust
from which he came and to which she'll soon return.
A handful of candles scented *Tranquility*, never lit.

His

White iPod and headphones, its playlist:
"Stairway to Heaven," "Devil with the Blue Dress On,"
oh anything by Phil Collins and Genesis.
Duct-taped black rim bifocals. *700 Club* golf tees.
Garden of Eatin' blue chips, mostly crumbs.
Camping photo in poncho and Angels cap.
Mel Gibson's *The Passion of the Christ*.
Fig-leaf boxers, XL. His bookie's wager:
$500 on a Cubs vs. Red Sox World Series 2004.
Your new Verizon phone # is 666–2480. Can you hear me now?
Her bra's left breast cookie. The *Sports Illustrated* Swimsuit Issue.
A few blue pills, Bud Light bottle, the morning's apple core.

This week's TO-DO LIST: Rake leaves into piles (check)
and ignite with angel's flaming sword (check).
Rename bears and bulls and blackhawks (check).
E-mail Cain, the wanderer (check). Update Will and Trust.

Ike's Caddy

I

This conspiracy of greens: not simply the primly-clipped Bermuda grass
    but cash tips,
plaid pants, those teas with dear Mamie whose own boy had grown
    too old for it.
Then country club summers, assorted polyester blazers, pink Cadillacs,
    and the caddy shack
only a little less wacked than the one Bill Murray banked millions on.
    Born lucky,
son of a Secret Service agent who yawned through Ike's lawn-dawdling
    Gettysburg retirement,
the kid bagged a job lugging Ike's bag, feathery leather emblazoned
    with the presidential seal
whose arrows Ike wished he'd shot on No. 9 instead of the 3-wood
    sliced deep into sawgrass rough.
One caddy, five guys with ten guns, and Ike tempering his temper.

There's talk of Nixon, Khrushchev, Kennedy's Bay of Pigs blunder,
    then the plunder of assassination,
a world so unhinged anything might shoulder through its sprung door,
    maybe the old man
some nutcase's target. No sweat. Not to worry. Until Ike asked
    for the brass-bladed
Acushnet Bullseye putter his caddy had left beside seventeen's
    cracked plastic ballwasher.
Then walkie-talkies crackled, men in black Ban-Lons gunned
    golf carts flashing blue.
Ike holed his bogey. Applause, headshakes, a choral "Nice putt, sir."

In triumph Ike took the scenic route home to spy the corn's
        early August green,
shucking ears to prick plump kernels so sugared their milk eked
        down his thumb.
When a dusty Dodge pickup bucked to a stop, the farmer barked,
        "Whatcha doing there, mister . . . "—
and so arrested breath, agents hustling, the unfazed farmer's
        ". . . Mr. President?"
Then the caddy's muffled chuckle gave way to belly-laugh,
        his first act of diplomacy
ushering his second: the ritual exchange of a dozen ears
        for a dozen balls,
the farmer's faded overalls stuffed with souvenir tees
        and a poncho
the boss inscribed, "With deep thanks, from one vet to another."

            2
With college came other grass to water, feed, and cut.
        How strange
to pamper weed, not spray or pluck it. The seventies' smoke
        rewrote his three-act
Summer of Love into one big Happening so far out every
        conversation began
with ¿Que pasa, man? and each answer begged the question,
        "What's happening?"
For this, he quit the golf team and took up theater,
        reveling
in self-destruction aptly disguised as thespian-Zen
        self-actualization,
daft enough to kneel before peals of applause
        whose madness
even Law School's Nixonian appeal couldn't equal.

Why not off-Broadway, Hamlet in New York,
    oh, Tennessean
in lime green tights?—there to suffer the slings
    and arrows
of outrageous reviews and importunate landlords,
    Shakespearean stuff
a caddy hands Ike with his brass Bullseye putter, grip first.
    Don't condescend
to the guy he once was, a dopey guy. There's a dopey guy
    in each of us,
or a dopey girl resplendent in lace ruffles and pigtails.

When Mamie invited him to her New York hotel
    to swoon for
the actress he'd mooned over as a pheromonal teenager
    in love with
Sky King's Penny, he pinkied his cup, yes-ma'amed
    and smiled a lot
as if for the play's glossy 8 x 10 publicity shots.
    The mooned-over actress,
now ample with middle-age, amply *darlinged* him
    then touched
his too pink cheek. Act 1's rising action.

"Tell me, son, how's your father, mother, golf game,
    dog, and apartment?"
His answer, "Fine, fine, good, dead, and small."
    Act 2 begged
for a bit o' the Bard, so he obliged by palming a tea pot
    as prop
and flashing Danish flourish with a leap upon the tufted sofa.
    Then four hands
clapped as if four hundred, chit chat and crumpets with jam.
    Act 3.
Hugs bye-bye, Mamie clinching the shoulder-to-shoulder cinch
    lavender grandmas favor.

The actress so pressed her breasts against his chest he bumped
    a Chippendale table
outside the door whose purple curtain he didn't want to fall,
    no one there
to ask him if a wedge makes the green against this stiff breeze.

    3
Having kept Ike's score and kept it secret, a caddy's duty.
    Having served as confidante
to the President, if only a genial ex-pres, hair-tousled by
    the hand of power,
hand that tapped *it's a go* despite Normandy's bad weather.
    Having nearly lost
that beloved putter whose engraved italicized "Ike"
    upturned the sun.
Having played Hamlet, the bumbling stumbler's quest to be
    or not to be hungry,
not to be the hick N.Y. chicks make fun of, no matter
    his tights
and that skull he spoke to on stage and off, asking
    big questions
of grease paint, klieg lights, and rats in the kitchen's
    lone cupboard—
whiskered brothers of whispered desires.

Having sipped tea with a First Lady who slipped him
    grocery money
he splurged on booze and underwear. Having mashed
    the crushed-on actress
and felt that feast of adolescence come late in a hallway
    hung with mirrors
he saw it all doubled in. Having that and now this, this
    present tense dervish search
for an elevator that'll bring him down, *must* take him down
    from this pinnacle,

this rush only the cynical would begrudge, this effervescent
     fleetingly evanescent crest—
what, he wonders, might ever deflate this blissful instant?
     You there,
take your finger off that button. He'll find it soon enough,
     or it'll find him.
Ah, he's green, a dopey guy—beautifully, dangerously human.

Talk Radio

American men, once glum monks of silence,
whine like the puppy at a locked porch door.

Blue Tuesday

I want to invent a thing as beautiful and useless as the Slinky.
Because it's Blue Tuesday, second Tuesday of February,
a tradition invented by my mother who's fond of puzzlers,
say, Did the first inventor invent the notion of "new

and improved"?, or Given a philosophical tree's falling
in unpeopled woods, was there sound? Class dismissed.
Because it's Blue Tuesday I want to be Richard James
and wife Betty, all pumps and pearls, tinkering

a machine to harness ships' horsepower when *plink*
a spring skitters out and walks down the laboratory's
metal steps. Aha, they burped, over meatloaf lunch,
indigestion the mother of invention. The Slinky's pure

sprung pleasure. It doesn't feed nor clothe nor house
the poor, but it won't put your eye out either.
I have, in a fit of wayward fatherliness, spent all afternoon
walking a Slinky up the stairs so my daughter

could walk it down again. Good boy. The Slinky's
inventor invented this, too, a game to be played
by willing surrogates like you and me— not unlike
pilot Charles Sweeney, the unlucky surrogate

who delivered Oppenheimer's invention to Nagasaki,
Fat Man the first bomb he ever dropped.
That was 1945, same year the Slinky's invented.
If a plane drops a bomb that no one hears

and afterwards there's no one left, did it happen?
I too have ridden the moral high horse,
fingering Sweeney even more than Tibbets
who banked over Hiroshima not knowing

what mushroom would sprout. Sweeney knew,
and never the sour apple of regret. He didn't
sing the Blues, though both the singing
and the not are original American art forms,

the way "I want" becomes the Blues when
a chorus answers, "You can't have it!"
Sweeney, because it's Blue Tuesday,
second Tuesday of the second month,

coldest but shortest, metaphor of the human,
I wish I'd invented the Slinky. I wish you and I
were beautiful and useless together, dropping a big
fat Slinky from the blue sky of never happens.

In Human Hands

Once I admired the hand for the violence it could do
but mostly doesn't,

the apple tree for the fruit it sets
then gives away—

one for restraint,
the other for generosity we're not known for.

I lived the abyss between reach
and grasp,

inferring therefrom the necessity
of forgiveness.

This, the wager one makes in Confession,
whose supplication's less atonement than fear,

the better reason to beg a blessing—
fear of what we've yet to do, will do,

as it is now and ever shall be, world without end,
Amen.

That's why it's easy to lose count,
one bead nearer to hell or heaven, who knows?

There's all that kneeling, the purple robes,
a cross and someone nailed to it.

The story goes like this: one human hand held a spike,
the other a big hammer. A question swung

in the balance, and the man's hands
answered for us. *Yes,* he nailed,

yes yes yes. We'd kill anything,
even our gods.

Two

To Balance

Without you, nothing earthly stands firm. In our infancy
        and then our dotage, you dispense
           a fickle gift so toddlers' bottoms suffer your truancy
and later the assembled old folks broken-hip-kiss

their nursing home's linoleum. In ancient myth
        the hero disdains you. She leaps from a cliff
          into an ink well, or he, wielding his pocketknife,
slays the ill-mannered dragon. Aristotle straddled your roof

to found his theory of art, giving us pleasure
        and a lesson in you, good cop/bad cop.
        In matters of heart it's the lack of you men treasure
in their lovers, impetuous and thus prodigally hip,

reckless enough to sun topless on the noon deck.
        In marriage they look for you in bank book
        and bed sheets, woman who'll fund an IRA but yank
the blinds shut with her toes, oh Madonna-trick

men ask blondes to be. In politics moderates sip
        your apple juice then ride the centrists' hobbyhorse,
        though Rush scorned your charms for a wilder trip,
popping OxyContin to fuel his immoderate course

along ire's high wire. In games of chance gamblers fleece
        those who disdain you, pocketing the lost stash,
        then booze all night till someone bleats
how politely you've hailed closing time's last

Yellow Cab. Without you, I couldn't ride my bike,
          wear the funny shorts, the helmet that cracked
     when gravel showed me horizontal's what it's like
to be without you. As a kid I learned you while I walked

in my father's arms and later when his hands
          steadied the red Schwinn, prestidigitating away my fear.
     Invisible thus godlike, you arrived as if from the clouds—
then the letting go, and me impossibly pedaling on air.

Postcard to Henry James

Having a wonderful time. Wish you were here this April day you'd probably dub "lugubrious," Mr. James, you who wished to be the ascotted adjective, a clause's strawberries and whipped cream, tweed you cleaned with a horsehair brush while dictating to an amanuensis sentences as endless as this Illinois horizon, prairie punctuated here-there by a silo and that blackbird net tossed upon just-tilled dirt as darkly glistening as they, so one disappears, *poof*, like that, into the other's black magic.

"Like that," I nod to the boy in red cap snapping his fastball. We're talking but not. "Playing catch writes a good, long sentence," itself a sentence I'm thinking as the ball pops my mitt, thinking of thinking, thinking then this *pop* conjoins us toss to toss, son to father to father's father, both the lineage and my thinking of it Jamesian in theory if not practice, the whole of it Midwestern and not a miscreant's manor in sight.

Of this, Mr. James, you'd ask me to write down "how blackbirds halo the little orchard, angels in mind not body, how the shadow of wings drops morning's ancient history onto our shoulders, how these seraphs in dark disguise will not halt their flight nor hang high garlands when we die, each of us alone on the petaled sheet"—yours a death sentence longer though less swaying than the high hard one my son has flung into the arms of a young plum redolent with bloom. Dear Henry, this poem's for American youth. See, its blossoms cascade white magic onto your hair. See, *abracadabra,* just like that, your bald spot's gone.

Capitalism

Inventing something's only half the matter.
Then, the naming. For professionals of American
automobile marketing, this means a living coming up
with Mustang, Astrovan, Escalade—meal tickets
of chrome and rubber ego enhancement.

Imagine the failure of imagination that christened
my car the *850,* a number only engineers get lubed by.
Across its dash I've stacked brochures selling places
my Volvo can take me, say, Seattle's Giant Shoe Museum,
a site so grand it's "measured in yards of feet."

There's the east coast's Museum of Bad Art
in West Roxbury, Massachusetts, a gallery
where this poem might land a not-so cherished spot.
If my gas money lasts, I'll swing by the national
Museum of Jurassic Technology, pathetic oxymoron,

or the Museum of Questionable Medical Devices,
which should be but isn't next door to Houston's
Museum of Funeral History. With luck it's on to
the Museum of Beverage Containers, open weekdays
in Goodlettsville, Tennessee, where I might find

the coin operated coffee and cocoa machine
whose button I'd push and pray a cup slid down
before the stream of steaming liquid puddled
on concrete floor, work boots wet with disappointment.
On break at Container Corporation of America,

I quaffed industrial coffee with the not-yet-old men
my father went to war with. "Stay in school, kid,"
they'd night-shift whisper above the cup's curled lip.
Surely one survivor of The Greatest Generation
invented the coin-operated coffee machine,

dripping nostalgic for the foxhole java he sipped
after Iwo Jima fell. Grunts raised the flag on Suribachi—
once for real, once to sell newspapers. That's capitalism
his buddies died for: the pleasures of break room and
highway rest stop, your cup of joe no bargain at any price.

A Day's Work

Good intentions proffer one vice of the easily fleeced,
a tenet of Colonialism jowly Prince Charlie must've cursed
touring Bob Marley's Trench Town 'hood,
paunchy white guy sweating woolish tweeds,
the sheep in sheep's clothing. I always loved
those cartoons where the wolf and Ralph his sheepdog buddy
punch-in at the same lame time clock,
amiably glazed before the day's histrionics
a la my foreman and I at the box-making factory.
Long Don owned the clock's ticktock,
the horn that burped *let's work*, and my weekly check
handcuffed by taxes and a car payment. It's good work
if you can get it, this being Prince and heir
to the Teutonic-English electric chair,
no matter the dead princess or the frog-faced mistress
or a butler who claims he squeezed your toothpaste tube
as metaphor for indiscretions the British press
won't yet tattle. When Bob's widow Rita passes
Charles her Trench Town gift, it's no doobie
but a Rastafarian knit hat with fake dreadlocks,
so he dons it, dutifully, wearing his royal smirk.
The crowd inhales a collective Jah gasp,
seeing just this once not cold stone
but Charles's stoned beneficence,
Rita bonging the mic's lip with her own,
"Bob would burn a big, big spliff to this."
With rushed sobriety the Prince doffs his hat,
only a costume, and momentary at that,
like my Tennessean pal's playing Hamlet.

It's all in a day's work, as it was
at the factory where Alphonso Toss,
Jamaican machine-mate, lifted night shift's cross
upon his shoulders and hauled us aloft.
My good deed carpooled him to work,
but first to Southtown Cleaners where a rack
clack-clacked his jacket from back to front,
each pocket bagged with good weed.
No, no, children, I said "good deed."
Hey, demon of piece-rate contentment,
hey, angel of the boss's nightly discontent,
we twins cleaved to a cleaving machine.
I read Whitman while he cleaned
rope, an act of three-dimensional magic that suggests
my not-thereness at work, so there's your economic justice.
For his life's work my young son swore he'd corral
a job helping others and thereby earn "a big celery,"
which may feed but not clothe him in any traditional sense,
the way Roman soldiers' *salarium argentum* was paid in salt only,
as most of us used to but no longer earn a day's salary
by the sweat of our once sun-baked brows.

Song of the Night Shift Foreman

"His men" he called us, though one among us
    wore a dress, this prize Don eyed on the prowl.

Overtime he doled like lollipops to tots, his dollop of patronage,
    and then whatever he asked with the broom handle.

Over the slitter's whir and shush, paper's hiss across
    the block-long press, belch of forklift's bottled gas,

we his merry men sang our B-movie. At quarter to clock out,
    we bellowed songs, off-key and drunk from supper,

our insubordinates' anthem for Don
    trilled to The Beatles' "Come Together"—

    "Here come old squint-eye,
        he come grooving up slowly,
    he got juju eyeball,
        he got funky hairlip,
    he got nose down below his knees.
        Got to be a foreman,
    he just do what he please.
        Come together, right now, over Don."

This verse, alas, Don overheard the night he forgot
    his yellow foam earplugs. Hell hath no fury

like a scorned foreman, misery that passes for a joke
    among those who live by piecework,

200 boxes to the hour or your rear's hauled out.
    Hard by the clock, hard by the metal box

where you smoke 'em if you got 'em, Don slipped
    the steward a wad and fingered Bunsy come here,

broom handle palmed and sweaty. "There's ten men
    who'll take your job, if you won't do it."

On Thinking of the Second Time
They Shoveled Up Mr. Lincoln

*In September 1901, years after thieves
nearly made off with President Lincoln's
body from Oak Ridge Cemetery, Spring-
field, Illinois, his casket was disinterred
and reburied beneath tons of concrete.*

I

The first time I thought of the second time
I blood-cold rushed, arm wrestling
wet logs and newspaper wads,
the morning's bevy of war and pestilence
banking my fire's oak, its reeking elm.
The woodstove purred, fat Tom Cat
asleep amidst slant sunlight,
shadows at half mast. Late April's
late snow cast death in the role
of fool poet's "sweet, sweet repose."

What's behind that door?

2

Then my shovel's smacking stone
beneath the lilies' conspiracy,
rock as pocked as the yearbook photo
I've claimed is misnamed—
Oh no, that's not me, baby!,
a notion the spirit Lincoln must've felt
when scheming thieves shoveled up his body.
Those ghoulish fools figured $200,000 an ample ransom
for The Great Emancipator's corpse, then nearly stole away
before cops arrived to clamp the irons. Clink, clink.

No wonder the government wondered,
"Is that Lincoln in there?"

3

It's my faucet's incessant dribble,
third time I thought of Lincoln's second,
and how, too, the feds sent for plumbers
to solve their problem: "Misters Hopkins and Willey,
bring your tools. We've a job for you."
Potato soup bubbled on the stove, Monday's lost lunch,
then their bay mare's balky step, oil lamps and tall hats.
"Good sirs," Hopkins stuttered, awash in crypt light,
"you want me to open it?"

One minute the widow Smith's clogged drain,
the next a presidential coffin.

4

After that it's whiskey's work—conjuring
the *kerchunk* of plumber's chisel, *kerchunk* of lead,
dank *kerchunk* as the casket lid gave way.
"Now, look in there, Hopkins."
The plumber flinched above his cut six-inch square.
Below it, yellow mold stalagmites spritzed the broadcloth suit,
the starched shirt dust laden but spectral white.
The dead man's walnut knuckles had split seamed leather,
one final rebellion. (Lincoln so hated gloves
he drew them off when the Mrs. turned away.)

This, his tryst with eternity?

5

"What say you, Hopkins?"—this nation's question.
He nagged his nephew to fetch the whiskey.
Cork echoed, a swig, spooks feathered his lamp.
In that light, Hopkins cranked his face toward the man's
dusted with undertaker's chalk, powdered bronze,
their noses nearly touching.

In that light, he eyed what on earth becomes of us.
Then the beard. *The* beard.
In that sepulchral light, dead but not,
Hopkins uttered his line one first last time.

"It's him."

Pre-Bowdlerized Version of Poem for
a Fourth-Grade Illinois History Text

When you squirm upon your plastic desk chair,
you finger-flip the pages of this book of place
and someone's history. Yours? When you stare
daydreams upon the schoolroom's window, it's your face
glaciers scour clean and etch rivers upon,
your fine face flowered with yellows and blue.
When you swim June's chill stream, your day's fun
paddles Jolliet and Marquette's canoes
to sell their faith where rivers run.
When you rise and skip across the noon room,
you plant your soles where the Illinois grew
fat squash and beans in the dirt's fertile loam,
built great longhouses and wigwams too,
tended the villages that were their homes
until settlers' wagons heaved and hewed
the primeval forest, until square-jawed men
sunk plows in prairie grass ripped like cotton
when the steel cut through. Hear it? When you begin
to remember those others have forgotten—
the Peoria, Cahokia, and all who died
on The Trail of Tears—will you take this blame
for your own? Will you think Chicago's sky-
scrapers cloud the freedom Mr. Lincoln claimed
is yours, no matter the color of skin or eye?
When you, our little citizen, sit down to eat
your dinner's sweet corn, steak, and apple pie,
will you think this place your home, your feet
settled no matter the distance traveled?
Chapter One: History's not what happens to us.
History's who happens to tell the story. Unraveled,

each thread shows someone's *was* became another's *is*.
So off to bed with you. Float the pillowed blue.
Stars above you blink their blank promises,
then wink and become tomorrow, as will you.

CR5115STD *Responds to the*
National Consumer Survey

*Answer as many product and brand name
questions as possible. You may answer for
anyone in your household. Completion
of the survey is NOT a requirement for
Sweepstakes entry or Prize Redemption.*

Someone in this household enjoys (Casino Gambling),
(QVC Shopping), and (Self-Improvement).
Someone else enjoys (Do-It-Yourself).
Someone in this household uses (Caress Liquid Body Wash),
another prefers (Gillette). My (2) tabbies,
age (5–8), no longer respond to catnip.
They prefer (IAMS) to Meow Mix with Liver.
They are black and white. They have long tails.
They purr when sleeping with me.
His (1) (neutered) mutt prefers (table scraps)
to Purina Dog Chow. He has fleas.
I shop and save (Kroger) Double-Coupon Tuesdays.
Each week my household consumes (12+) Diet Pepsi,
(4–6) Ensure, (1) Sustacal, (1) Pepto-Bismol.
My household has a septic system.
Yes, I'd like info on maintaining it.
In this household someone desires (Weight Loss).
He wears (eyeglasses) and enjoys (hunting/shooting).
I read (12+) Romance books per year.
He reads (1) Science Fiction.
In this household I collect (porcelain dolls)
and he collects (NASCAR) die cast cars.
Someone in my household plans to buy
a (bass boat) and a (15+ ft.) RV.
No one invests or plans to invest
in stocks or mutual funds.
Someone in this household listens

to (Rush Limbaugh). Someone watches
(Oprah), who can't keep her weight off either.
We contribute to (Animal) charities.
Yes, enter my name in the preferred group
eligible to receive FREE SAMPLES,
VALUABLE COUPONS,
and assorted SPECIAL OFFERS.
No, nobody in this household is now or ever has been
a member of the (Democrat) party.

Post-Feminist Machismo

He fears women as well as men—worrying what befalls
his spear in the Venus Fly Trap of her power, beguiling as a fist.

Poet's Genie

"Forget *his* humdrum wishes.   What of mine?"
she complains, the one who   waits, a last rumpled sheet,
bottom of the flapjack stack   he writes upon.
Awaits his hand to say this   or that among dust mites
and dog hair, the contrite note   not sent, his usual harem
of unread memos. Waits beneath   the week's bleak
Dickinsian knock-offs, a slew of   true-false tests
pilfered from History's ash bin.   Beneath the Psychic's
fiddle-faddle warning: Do Not   Be Blind to Your Fate!
She waits in darkness, as do all   genies, bottled or not.
When chance doles what she'd   cajoled, night's little black dress
undone and lightning zippering   down, thunder's heartbeat
thrumming the blue vein behind   that pale veil,
his hand a storm upon her body.   Even then, ingrate
or insatiate, called to give him   what he wants,
half of her pouts, *Don't touch*.   The other, *Use me up*.

48

Parakeet and Dark Star

Equally unpredictable and uncommon,
one of them dropped from a Tree of Heaven
onto my calloused index finger, feathered
abandon tamed by hunger and the coming frost.

A miracle, my mother wept, while neighbors
trundled from clapboard houses to witness
who'd come to visit among shuttered factories
and a refinery belching dyspeptic American dreams.

Whose dream? Hope's a thing with wings
says the poet, her wings clipped by circumstance
and a minister's black veil, so the bird lived with me
for the price of seeds and astonishment.

At Fifth and Lincoln, his cage lay within mine.
The window perch, cuttlebone, and song,
even a tinny silver bell he'd beak-ring
until I'd let him fly the living room, small space

within the larger, within the great expanse
whose ends no one knows until the light itself
is whistled home to rest upon a finger,
the closed door opened then shut.

Mowing the Lawn

Putt putt, I ride on fossil fuel, the juice of fern and leaf,
the muck of once-was. Putt putt, I warm our globe
one green acre at a time. As a boy, I mowed without gas power
as does my buddy Dean. Green Dean. Back then as now
it was economics not ecology. Have you priced a hybrid?

I pushed, I sweated, I earned a man's allowance,
not unlike Tag, the bow-legged Japanese gardener
who plucked the lawn's eyebrows for my grandmother,
she of blue hair and lace gladiolas terraced along
the terra cotta porch. She of the voice that curdled milk.

Tuesdays he made landfall, hurricane of shears and clippers,
toting the lone mower he'd not so much push as chase.
Tag had no time for lost time, though just to be sure
the war-time feds interned him to save us from the Japs
he wasn't. The Republic's no match for paranoia.

Once, chasing the Wiffle ball of my World Series,
I spilled over Tag yanking weeds beside the arched porch
trellised with trumpet creeper and the strumming
of hummingbird wings, thrum of this world,
his knees keeping the porch safe for democracy.

That good man sang foreign to me and I got scared—
as kids will. But I didn't care—as kids won't,
I please wanted my ball please, which he found
amidst a clutch of dandelions he'd turn to wine.
Come winter he sipped the bittersweet of our fear.

Three

Appetites Earthly and Other

Slower is better they say of love-making
and fine dining, best among our many appetites,
so I'm pleased to have reached too late
for the last slice, pepperoni and black olives
I can say to have refused, my little white lie.

I can say as well to have lifted my hand
in a gesture of great magnanimity
that also raised my eyes from plate to window
where night moths feed on light, this at least half right.
They plink against the glass, embrace the screen,

wanting wanting wanting the heavenly bulb they'd
cook themselves upon. Such appetite for light
St. Augustine suffered, as did perhaps that fellow
who shot the abortion doctor and those whom
Allah calls to detonate themselves among children.

Between want and refusal, which makes us human?
I'm thinking of the Atlas moth, wingspan nearly a foot,
who's born without a mouth. It's true she's done
all her eating in the larva stage, a state I find myself
perpetually in, always about to become something better.

To hasten and guide this process, Augustine suggests,
straight-faced, *orate sine intermissione,*
"pray without interruption," a state of continual about-to-be
he thinks unlikely to foment trouble,
though what of "shot" and "detonate" above?

What would I become without appetites
or mouth to satisfy them? Whose table would I share,
whose bed? Surely a time will come when sleep
pleases more than sex, when even pizza loses
its primal appeal, as it did for my uncle Sandy

burdened with muscular dystrophy and a wife
who'd not change his diapers. As it did then, too,
for my mother, who spooned the puree
her brother's wilted throat aborted down chin and bib.
My mother who wouldn't eat when he could not.

Aesthetics of Desire

    I

I love the way things open,
the fervid shudder and release that breathes *relinquish*,
a lover tonguing your ear.

    2

I'm student of boxtop flap and lip,
of wine cork and the synthetic plugs it doesn't pay to sniff,
even beer cans' blustery history from tin to steel to aluminum
and the corollary evolution of pull tab to pop top.

    3

Our lips' apt parting beckons other partings
as *un-* undoes clasp, button, zip—prefix as prequel
to the fated tale of man and woman: lips open, those big gates
slammed shut.

    4

Every Man She Kisses Dies, shouts today's tabloid headline,
and still no shortage of suitors for Maria Teresa Hemlock Lips
of Loveland, Colorado, pun intended.
One smooch and gone: car wreck, heart attack, wild dogs of Borneo—
something smacks them down quick after their lips smack.
Truth is, each lover we kiss dies in some lost hour,
not to mention us.

5
So the variable's not *if* but *when*,
Tuesday noon's Civil Defense siren chides—
a notion giving birth to the smorgasbord and the 30–pack Pabst.
The Grateful Dead sang "too much of everything is just enough,"
so the genie pops out and we complain,
"Just *three* wishes?!"

6
Change is what we're after, a manner of opening
not unlike Thoreau's Walden year,
or for that matter not unlike his tale of the beetle who emerges
from a kitchen table's apple-wood.
Who'd refuse "the beautiful and wingéd life unexpectedly come forth
at last"?

7
What age a woman blooms full come-hither
is something men argue over fire and beer.
How the middle-aged and divorced adduce it's twenty-eight.
The Opening and The Ending.
How married guys add ten years in self-defense.
Whose petal wilts alone?

8
I love milkweed redolent with dew, the bee's drunken knock knock.

9
A year maybe two past twenty-eight, my wife's rose opened,
high on high noon's ample pollen.

10

Wise up, boys. There's the nectar of then
and the nectar of now-again, sweeter because few.
Ahead there's August's long hour, its heat lightning,
its green gone over. There's seed aloft
in the wind's electric resurrection.

Natural Selection

Saying some words makes us feel dirty
but powerful,
so we survive and multiply.

Words to boast or threaten,
to enflame or to belittle,
"belittle" both metaphor and low blow.

Words pubescents slumber-party giggle
then quick do each other's hair,
"do" itself a verb to make girls blush.

Words boys strut across the stage
of adolescent Greek theatre,
conjuring their fathers' tragic swagger.

Words women spout when phoning
the divorce lawyer, or whisper while ogling
the leather-chapped hard hat stud

erecting the ladies' room door,
that circus bigtop of adjectives.
Now's the time to say these words silently to yourself.

Saying them makes us feel powerful
but dirty,
culture helpless against the gold rush of Natural Selection.

"Calling it *Darwinism*," claims E. O. Wilson,
"is a rhetorical device to make evolution seem not fact
but mere faith, like Maoism."

Repeat that silently to yourself.
Me? I'd thought to say them out loud,
these words totemic

as the testosterone they unleash.
You wanted to hear them spoken
as the word was made flesh.

These the father of spear and hunt
and lust. These the proud daddy
of our H-bomb

and their videotaped beheadings.
These words make reason shudder
as if before a god.

Religion

Human fear and the rules of grammar demand *and*
to suggest something comes after.

Upon the Porch Swing's Time Machine

You with the yellow bonnet,

      with hair that would be gold

if gold were hair,

      come swing upon

these freshly painted slats,

      our throne bolt-through

with gleaming chain, a link

for each blink-and-squint Sunday we'll sit beneath.

      Look, the rust's all gone,

      nest droppings too,

the fledglings flown if not the coop

then porch to locust forest.

Come swing our 1919,

      the Great War over, the Second not yet,

and that bomb, The Bomb,

still a genie in Oppenheimer's knickers.

It's noon lemonade,

a pitcher and tall glasses,

and no one's mama

has yet birthed AIDS or Osama,

the drive-by shooting, crystal meth, or the Internet.

You there, with bonnet and parasol,

let's bamboozle the fool gods of our hour,

and by our swinging say a thing

bodies in motion know:

history's pendulum hangs

not from heaven—that clock's broken—

but from a daft rafter of our own making.

To My Hair

In youth, I undervalued you, as I did my father
            who grew smarter as you grew thinner. In truth,
        I mistreated you: ball cap, helmet, summer buzz.

In the after-practice shower you bore bar soap's indignity:
            pink Palmolive, deodorant Dial, the sodden leprechaun
        jigging his Irish Spring. I lied to you, swearing
I'd never scissor your split ends.

Thus you ride the waves of my hormonal ocean,
            as lately I've pampered you with *Cationic Vegetal Protein*
        and fruit acids to strengthen the cuticle, root of beauty.

I've rinsed with *revitalizing Vitamin E and B3,*
            slathered handfuls of *B5 to amplify and refresh you,*
        to empower a healthy sheen and boost your daily resiliency.
All the bottles say it's so!

From this costly, extravagant effort, what have we gained?
            My ears loom hirsute mittens,
        my eyebrows woolly caterpillars.

I do not mourn you, victim of phlegmatic genetics.
            The comb-over's a ventriloquist whose lips flap.
        I'm poster child for male pattern baldness
because Propecia sounds uglier than bald looks.

Because mine shaved like Jordan's is all bumps and knob.
            Because sheep glands keep me up at night, counting.
        Because Rogaine grows fuzz but leaves a lusty eunuch.

Because to mourn you brings lethargy and depression
        that problematize the likelihood of scoring anyway.
    Because spray-on hair ravages our fragile ozone layer.
Because, dear already-lost and soon-to-be,

I sweat my fifty sit-ups after lunch
        and munch carrots in lieu of Ben & Jerry's.
    Because my wife tousles what's left of you then kisses me hard.

Lovesong Ending with (   )

Wittgenstein, that brilliant blowhard,
           says one can say only so much and not
    all, language a kind of cage.
"But hey, Tiger," his book says,
           "throw yourself against the cage wall.
Go ahead, my wild lion, my PetSmart kitten."
           So *this* and *this* and *this* I say
    with my articulate shoulder,
           my oratorical hip and back,
and *that* and *that*, too, with a rhetorical forehead.
           But my body just earns bruise bars,
    each saying *stupid, stupid.* Listen,
           I'll keep blowing this world's harmonica,
    a tune for the short of breath.
Short of breath is the worst kind of short,
           worse than a kid's not reaching
                his top shelf cookies
    or later the scotch priced with red numbers.
Numbers are also a kind of cage,
           unless one believes in infinity
or heaven. Say, seven, a start to the week,
           and twelve, as in the apostles,
and three three three—a triple trinity
or three times one hundred eleven. By this means
           factors make up numbers as syllables do words,
    my love, let me count the ways,
and sometimes words make up words,
           as in *blow* and *hard*, or *harmonic* and *a—*
           a, our indefinite article's
    shrewd way to live in this world:
           sure of nothing but loving what's here,
a zinnia, *a* frost, *a* kiss. *A* lovesong.

Sometimes things get definite (insert *the* above)
       or worst of all possessive (insert *my* above).
    That makes of love something almost but no.
       Thanks, the door says by closing. Enough.
Even cages have doors. Our lips say (   )

At the Mountain Man Rendezvous in
Fairplay, Colorado

Everything plays dress-up at high altitude. South Park
          levitates in wavery heat, sky cobalt and unbroken
    atop Mt. Silverheels, sage lavish in brief bloom.

Beside a tan canvas teepee, Chiefs Long Hare
          and Running Bare, splendid in period attire,
    explain their names to a curious Japanese tourist

flashing some digital state-of-the-art as teensy
          as his wife shy in stars and stripes sunglasses.
    One doe-eyed maid braids hemp purses,

her body twig thin in hand-stitched deer skin
          and those shoulders her papoose is strapped over,
    a Pekinese with sad eyes and one apt feather.

At this elevation, a suspendered gent saws his fiddle
          while dance hall girls jig then stop to swig a jug
    propped and corked with grace their feet can't mimic.

Pine fires pop, mutts sniff the air and drool, beads
          around their lank necks. My wife pow-wows with
    Make-Believe-in-Loin-Cloth, warrior-accountant,

his beard as deftly carved as the stone tomahawk
          that doubles as his peace pipe. The wind rises
    and so does she, feet levitating on wavery heat,

her eyes cobalt and sky. At this elevation,
          she's blue lupine's peppery scent. She's
    buttercup, paintbrush, and prairie smoke.

She's fawn lily, yellow bell, and forget-me-not.
　　　　She's daisies in the window box. I'm dressed
　　as young love, the dizzy quick breath of high altitude.

Inverse Aviary, in Which Birds Talk

Why praise the first robin,

    and not the last to leave?

The one who dawdles

    till ice has cracked

the bird bath.

Issa, himself on wing,

    late and alone,

    once told a bird:

That the world's going to end someday

    doesn't concern you.

    It's time to build your nest,

    you build your nest.

But when it's time to leave, he asked,

    what then?

    "I'll know," the last robin said,

"when snow dapples my wings

    as gray does your hair."

Then the last robin feasted on

tossed burnt toast,

he sipped from an icy scrim—

sun's parting gift.

What of the next place?,

Issa asked.

"So,"

the last robin answered,

black-eyeing the fretted sky,

these leaves unhinged,

an eyelash of frosted grass.

"So what."

On Reading 'Prince Valiant' in the Sunday Comics

This strip's demographic is geriatric, old folks
piloting a Hover-'Round across Retirement Valley
from the land where narrative's doled in weekly
installments. Nowadays, who has patience for dallying?

Before Instant Messenger and the cable news scene,
before ubiquitous wireless and a text-messaging thumb,
the mind craved sequential chapters one-two-*fini*.
Back then a sound byte spun leisurely at 33 1/3 rpm.

Back then, a stack of the kids' 45s drove them crazy,
the stereo as bulky as the casket they've prepaid proper
at the corner mortuary, all the boss platters given way
to hymns, "On Eagle Wings" the chart-topper.

Prince Val would complain the nursing home's
America's last bastion of chivalry, the aged and off-track
forgetting names but not their manners. Ahem,
back in the day, one always fingered the right fork,

opened a door for the lady, and surely did not mack
in public. Now, we're serfs to one dark fiefdom or another—
Hollywood's or Pat Roberston's—a perpetually slack
though moral tug-of-war Val would slice asunder.

Each Sunday's tale is Arthur and those tabled knights,
Val's wife Aleta, lovely lass of the Misty Isles. And Arn,
who takes up dad's good fight, whatever the fight.
Neither intemperate sea serpent nor off-the-wagon dragon

musses Val's coiffeur, the Singing Sword wreaking havoc
upon rabid clans of Visigoths and Vandals keen
to pillage as lustily as Lee Harvey Oswald sacked America.
This one's *Our Story*: The chronicles report Lewis Hanson

piloted Air Force One to Dallas, delivering JFK to history,
Jackie sporting the pink pillbox hat. They say
Hanson shared TV dinners and chit chat at his blustery
mother-in-law's table, savoring Jack's weekly heroic segue.

To be continued. Gentle reader, this fable's next Sunday's telling.
You can't wait to hear how Colonel Hanson chokes down
Cronkite's televised news. How Camelot, falling,
our fond myth, collapses in bitter gravy of the modern . . .

Slippery Slope

Everything's on it, the Big Conscience cautions,
   what with The Man smoking our privacy rights,
      science embracing cloning, and the music industry
         losing its means of distribution and thus monopoly,
            that most American of anti-American ideologies.

         Was the Golden Age our fathers'? Was it Roman or Greek
         or the caved domain of that hirsute chap toting a club?
      How old, then, the good old days? Gray hairs,
   we warn it's a collective moral undoing:
W's second term, a chain of French McDonalds,

the absent back seat of NASCAR's Viagra ride.
   Everybody's got a gripe. But ethics flex
      stronger than you'd think. Stronger, for instance,
         than my own right arm dropping baseball for softball
            and then to coach, unable to turn the double play.

         It's personal and physical now. No more basketball,
         these knees and gravity's intimate acquaintance.
      Only the bike, on which I progressed from training wheels
   to 27 gears and alloy frame. Soon I'll slip back down
to fat tires and cushioned seat, a horn that burps, and then

to the lift chair in whose lap my father lifted off the planet.
   No, Chicken Little, it's not the sky that's falling nor us,
      if by us you mean the whole of you and me, a rabble,
         the dirty little *we*. Forget Prozac, opiate of the masses.
            Freedom's an iPod shuffling Lennon, Mozart, and Marley.

Colonialism

In the old America I knew a guy who ate glass—
exclusively beer pitchers and *ex post facto* his divorce—
impressing his buddies and enticing a throng of thonged
neon-lit lounge ladies with postmodern nihilistic bravado.

After all, killing the self's the epitome of nihilism,
an inverted Jim Jones Kool-Aid end-party,
believing so much in nothing you become it.

In the old America eating glass was metaphor
for post-colonial indigestion, though now even simile's
as unveiled as the veiled Death-to-America parade,
everyone beating himself happily bloody.

Recent studies show owning a dog adds years to one's life,
as does having but not owning a wife, a nuance of colonialism
eluding American men so their troubles become the ex-beloveds'.

In our nation's trophy case, there's a beer pitcher
featuring a half-moon bite. Its honored spot's beside
Marketing's Glamour Shots and the UN Team-Building's
Egg and Spoon Race second-place plaque, haloed by light.

Owning a thing's not the same as knowing it,
and knowing's a form of ownership fraught with peril.
In the old America I knew a guy who ate glass.

When sleeping alone, one's bed seems much bigger
(or is it colder?), a veritable three dog night, the schmaltzy band
who sang "one is the loneliest number" as if it were possible
to sleep alone in this world's Shah-sized brass bed.

Crickets amongst the roses can't carry the tune,
nor is Muzak sufficient to the task of somnambulating
the citizenry, no song amply soporific

to forestall the terrible angel on wing. Americans
no longer consider men with beards to be wise.
Behind us, history's bicep bulges blue, flexing
its fresh tattoo. It's Benjamin's Angel of History

and one star-struck horse shucking debris in want of
keeping up. Most days we're the horse, some days debris.
Detritus has "us" in it, and that ink's no cartoon joke.

Parable of the American Stag Party

Google "Candy Barr" and you'll get snickers,
   but not caramel, peanuts, and milk chocolate.
     At 16, Candy blushed as her dress peeled off,

demure in *Smart Alec*, the fab fifties' stag film—
   door knock, small talk, then lucky Alec
     forgetting to yank his black socks off.

Marx claims the body's a model of *commodity reification*.
   Women use it to make a buck, undressing for a fee
     while dancing to the band's boom-boom.

Men use it to make a point, strapping a svelte
   bomb belt around the Palestinian girl's belly, another
     lethal boom. Let us pray: the body is the devil's

weapon of choice. Ask the Reverend Samson
   after his televised fall from grace. Ask the Muslim
     woman darkly veiled. Ask the man why he veiled her.

Candy Barr made news and thus a living, shooting
   the drunk-beat-her-up husband just a little,
     bad press good for sales. Busted toking weed

she pending-appeal-seduced mobster Mickey Cohen,
   then wept for dead JFK and blubbered for lover
     Jack Ruby when he whacked Oswald among

the assembled white hats, the crescendo a weekend
   fling with the pre-Viagra Hefner—hers a rogues'
     symphony of modern American malehood.

In her honor, the Sexy Action News Team delivers
   horror perfectly coiffed, ties and rouge blood red,
      diagnosing us in need of ethical push-ups.

Though I never saw her naked or nearly so, *nearly*
   the illusion men come for, dollars in their fist of teeth,
      fantasy rides me into our long night.

Never mind she wasn't *my* wife or daughter,
   never mind the coarsening of digital culture.
      He without sin casts the first censor.

Arts of Joy

Now I have the Great Crested Flycatcher
amidst my Red Delicious, the tree's
spindly arm so freighted with apples
it sags under the bird's bird-weight
then springs at his departure
like the board just after a diver's flung up
and gone. *Weep weep weep*, he trills
from the overgrown fence row,
his three notes so laden with gravity
I wonder is this song or his lament,
one wing among the green going going?

And that, my friends, is how reason
insinuates its bone lonely self
among the arts of joy—the least of which
is knowing when to snip the string
that tethers us, our sky blue why.

The bird's after-image is more than
I can take, really, more than I can ask
of Wednesday's usual desultory coffers,
high noon offering its unspent zenith.
I want to say there's absolutely nothing
like this vision of bird and apples. I want
to say absolutely nothing else gives
of wings and fruit. Then I think of
nights my wife rose flushed above me—
this, the only store I put in absolutes.

Youthful Indiscretions

The usual excuses: Spring untethered its feathered pollen
    up my nose,
and forgive me, father, everyone else *was* doing it.
    Back then
I wanted to do my part to end the Vietnam War,
    so I bared my end
and waved the nation's frayed Old Glory—
    "Look," I said,
streaking youth's tragic logic across the smoke
    of Nixon's years,
the world unhinged as were my jeans and reason.

Cop cars jumped the curb but kissed white pines
    and thus
kissed our rears. We ran, as criminals do,
    imagining
the precarious political prisoner jailed in his
    nefarious buff.
My buddy, world's fastest white guy, didn't beat me
    to the van
we sprawled belly-up under, sorority girls pointing,
    cops' black flashlights
as dull as they—this, our great escape.

The riot squad plodded comic lockstep, thudding heads
    we'd laddered
into clouds. Our school, unranked on any scale,
    catapulted to #3

on *Playboy's* infamous Campus Streaking Poll,
        a heady blip
before fire hoses washed the starch out.
        America,
to be young and naked, to wear our best intentions
        like skin,
to erect an insurrection that flops. Is this not foreign policy?

My pal photographed a dour Nixon sulking sunny
        San Clemente beach
after the Prez died in office or resigned, pick your metaphor.
        Our act of conscience,
or lack thereof, hadn't brought the big man down,
        but those flicks
bought a turntable my friend bequeathed to me.
        America, if you need me,
I'm spinning the needle atop Grateful Dead LPs.
        I'm weeding a garden,
recycling, coaching my son to turn the double play.

America, you'll not hear from me. I'll not wave our flag
        nor burn it.
I'll not eat quiche or wear a beret, nor will I vote third party.
        America,
you can bank on me. I'll not top off my tank with Marxist
        Venezuelan oil.
Citizens, I promise you. I am rehabilitated.
        I will not run naked
through these streets again—unless today's war
        lingers
bloody and pointless as the last we swore was last.

Kevin Stein is the author of nine books, including *American Ghost Roses* (winner of the Society of Midland Authors Poetry Award), *Chance Ransom,* and *Bruised Paradise,* as well as two books of literary criticism and the poetry anthologies *Illinois Voices* and *Bread & Steel,* the latter an audio CD. Recipient of the National Endowment for the Arts Poetry Fellowship and *Poetry's* Frederick Bock Prize, Stein is Illinois Poet Laureate and Caterpillar Professor of English at Bradley University.

Illinois Poetry Series
Laurence Lieberman, Editor

Dear John, Dear Coltrane
Michael S. Harper (1985)

Poems from the Sangamon
John Knoepfle (1985)

In It
Stephen Berg (1986)

The Ghosts of Who We Were
Phyllis Thompson (1986)

Moon in a Mason Jar
Robert Wrigley (1986)

Lower-Class Heresy
T. R. Hummer (1987)

Poems: New and Selected
Frederick Morgan (1987)

Furnace Harbor: A Rhapsody of
   the North Country
Philip D. Church (1988)

Bad Girl, with Hawk
Nance Van Winckel (1988)

Blue Tango
Michael Van Walleghen (1989)

Eden
Dennis Schmitz (1989)

Waiting for Poppa at the
   Smithtown Diner
Peter Serchuk (1990)

Great Blue
Brendan Galvin (1990)

What My Father Believed
Robert Wrigley (1991)

Something Grazes Our Hair
S. J. Marks (1991)

Walking the Blind Dog
G. E. Murray (1992)

The Sawdust War
Jim Barnes (1992)

The God of Indeterminacy
Sandra McPherson (1993)

Off-Season at the Edge of the
World
Debora Greger (1994)

Counting the Black Angels
Len Roberts (1994)

Oblivion
Stephen Berg (1995)

To Us, All Flowers Are Roses
Lorna Goodison (1995)

Honorable Amendments
Michael S. Harper (1995)

Points of Departure
Miller Williams (1995)

Dance Script with Electric Ballerina
Alice Fulton (reissue, 1996)

To the Bone: New and Selected
   Poems
Sydney Lea (1996)

Floating on Solitude
Dave Smith (3-volume reissue,
   1996)

Bruised Paradise
Kevin Stein (1996)

Walt Whitman Bathing
David Wagoner (1996)

Rough Cut
Thomas Swiss (1997)

Paris
Jim Barnes (1997)

The Ways We Touch
Miller Williams (1997)

The Rooster Mask
Henry Hart (1998)

The Trouble-Making Finch
Len Roberts (1998)

Grazing
Ira Sadoff (1998)

Turn Thanks
Lorna Goodison (1999)

Traveling Light:
  Collected and New Poems
David Wagoner (1999)

Some Jazz a While:
  Collected Poems
Miller Williams (1999)

The Iron City
John Bensko (2000)

Songlines in Michaeltree:
  New and Collected Poems
Michael S. Harper (2000)

Pursuit of a Wound
Sydney Lea (2000)

The Pebble: Old and New Poems
Mairi MacInnes (2000)

Chance Ransom
Kevin Stein (2000)

House of Poured-Out Waters
Jane Mead (2001)

The Silent Singer:
  New and Selected Poems
Len Roberts (2001)

The Salt Hour
J. P. White (2001)

Guide to the Blue Tongue
Virgil Suárez (2002)

The House of Song
David Wagoner (2002)

X =
Stephen Berg (2002)

Arts of a Cold Sun
G. E. Murray (2003)

Barter
Ira Sadoff (2003)

The Hollow Log Lounge
R. T. Smith (2003)

In the Black Window:
  New and Selected Poems
Michael Van Walleghen (2004)

A Deed to the Light
Jeanne Murray Walker (2004)

Controlling the Silver
Lorna Goodison (2005)

Good Morning and Good Night
David Wagoner (2005)

American Ghost Roses
Kevin Stein (2005)

Battles and Lullabies
Richard Michelson (2005)

Visiting Picasso
Jim Barnes (2006)

The Disappearing Trick
Len Roberts (2006)

Sleeping with the Moon
Colleen J. McElroy (2007)

Expectation Days
Sandra McPherson (2007)

Tongue & Groove
Stephen Cramer (2007)

A Map of the Night
David Wagoner (2008)

Immortal Sofa
Maura Stanton (2008)

National Poetry Series

Eroding Witness
Nathaniel Mackey (1985)
Selected by Michael S. Harper

Palladium
Alice Fulton (1986)
Selected by Mark Strand

Cities in Motion
Sylvia Moss (1987)
Selected by Derek Walcott

The Hand of God and a Few
   Bright Flowers
William Olsen (1988)
Selected by David Wagoner

The Great Bird of Love
Paul Zimmer (1989)
Selected by William Stafford

Stubborn
Roland Flint (1990)
Selected by Dave Smith

The Surface
Laura Mullen (1991)
Selected by C. K. Williams

The Dig
Lynn Emanuel (1992)
Selected by Gerald Stern

My Alexandria
Mark Doty (1993)
Selected by Philip Levine

Use Trouble
Michael S. Harper (2009)

Sufficiency of the Actual
Kevin Stein (2009)

The High Road to Taos
Martin Edmunds (1994)
Selected by Donald Hall

Theater of Animals
Samn Stockwell (1995)
Selected by Louise Glück

The Broken World
Marcus Cafagña (1996)
Selected by Yusef Komunyakaa

Nine Skies
A. V. Christie (1997)
Selected by Sandra McPherson

Lost Wax
Heather Ramsdell (1998)
Selected by James Tate

So Often the Pitcher Goes to
   Water until It Breaks
Rigoberto González (1999)
Selected by Ai

Renunciation
Corey Marks (2000)
Selected by Philip Levine

Manderley
Rebecca Wolff (2001)
Selected by Robert Pinsky

Theory of Devolution
David Groff (2002)
Selected by Mark Doty

Rhythm and Booze
Julie Kane (2003)
Selected by Maxine Kumin

Shiva's Drum
Stephen Cramer (2004)
Selected by Grace Schulman

The Welcome
David Friedman (2005)
Selected by Stephen Dunn

Michelangelo's Seizure
Steve Gehrke (2006)
Selected by T. R. Hummer

Veil and Burn
Laurie Clements Lambeth (2007)
Selected by Maxine Kumin

Spring
Oni Buchanan (2008)
Selected by Mark Doty

Other Poetry Volumes

Local Men and *Domains*
James Whitehead (1987)

Her Soul beneath the Bone:
   Women's Poetry on Breast Cancer
Edited by Leatrice Lifshitz (1988)

Days from a Dream Almanac
Dennis Tedlock (1990)

Working Classics: Poems on
   Industrial Life
*Edited by Peter Oresick and
   Nicholas Coles* (1990)

Hummers, Knucklers, and Slow
   Curves: Contemporary Baseball
   Poems
Edited by Don Johnson (1991)

The Double Reckoning of
   Christopher Columbus
Barbara Helfgott Hyett (1992)

Selected Poems
Jean Garrigue (1992)

New and Selected Poems, 1962–92
Laurence Lieberman (1993)

The Dig and *Hotel Fiesta*
Lynn Emanuel (1994)

For a Living: The Poetry of Work
*Edited by Nicholas Coles and
   Peter Oresick* (1995)

The Tracks We Leave: Poems on
   Endangered Wildlife of North
   America
Barbara Helfgott Hyett (1996)

Peasants Wake for Fellini's *Casanova*
   and Other Poems
*Andrea Zanzotto; edited and
   translated by John P. Welle and
   Ruth Feldman; drawings by
   Federico Fellini and Augusto
   Murer*
   (1997)

Moon in a Mason Jar and *What My
   Father Believed*
Robert Wrigley (1997)

The Wild Card: Selected Poems,
   Early and Late
*Karl Shapiro; edited by Stanley
   Kunitz and David Ignatow* (1998)

Turtle, Swan and *Bethlehem in
   Broad Daylight*
Mark Doty (2000)

The University of Illinois Press
is a founding member of the
Association of American University Presses.

_____

Composed in 11/14 Adobe Garamond Pro
with Futura display
by Celia Shapland
at the University of Illinois Press
Designed by Copenhaver Cumpston
Manufactured by Cushing-Malloy, Inc.

University of Illinois Press
1325 South Oak Street
Champaign, IL 61820-6903
www.press.uillinois.edu